FISH

Mark Evans

B.Vet.Med.

DORLING KINDERSLEY

London • New York • Stuttgart

![DK]

A DORLING KINDERSLEY BOOK

Project Editor Liza Bruml
Art Editor Jane Tetzlaff
Editor Miriam Farbey
Photographers Paul Bricknell, Max Gibbs, Dave King
Additional Photography Jane Burton, Neil Fletcher,
Frank Greenaway, Colin Keates, Tim Ridley,
Kim Taylor, Jerry Young
Illustrator Malcolm McGregor

First published in Great Britain in 1993 by
Dorling Kindersley Limited, 9 Henrietta Street,
London WC2E 8PS

Colour reproduction by Colourscan, Singapore
Printed and bound in Italy by Arnoldo Mondadori, Verona

Models: Tony Arthurs, Jenny Baskerville, Oliver Baskerville,
Jacob Brubert, Maya Foa, Simon Gangadeen, Pete Hodson,
Natalie Lyon, Carlie Nicolls, Ben and Matthew Redmond

Dorling Kindersley would like to thank David Pool of Tetra
Information Centre; The Goldfish Bowl of Oxford;
Wildwoods Water Gardens Ltd and
Lynn Bresler for the index.

Picture credits: Oxford Scientific Films/John E Paling p10 ml;
Richard Davies of Oxford Scientific Films Ltd p15 bl; Bruce
Coleman Ltd/Michael Fogden p40 bl; ARPS/Peter Davey
p40 mr; Area London Ltd/Liz and Tony Bomford p42 br

Note to parents
This book teaches your child how to be
a caring and responsible pet owner. But
remember, your child must have your
help and guidance in every aspect of
day-to-day pet care. Don't let your child
keep fish unless you are sure that your
family has the time and resources to
look after them properly – for the whole
of their lives.

Contents

Introduction

The first step to becoming a fish-keeper is to choose the right kind and number of fish. Fish that live in cold water are the easiest to care for. In time, you will become a more experienced fish-keeper and will be able to look after warm-water fish. Whichever fish you have in your tank, you will need to look after them every day. Not just to start with, but for the whole of their lives.

Your pets' home
You can have a lot of fun planning a special home for your fish. It will be easier to make their tank interesting if you learn all about how fish live underwater. Try to find out the things they like to do.

Shopping basket full of things you will need

You can put plants in the gravel to make an underwater garden

Caring for your fish
You will only be your pets' best friend if you care for them properly. You will need to make sure that they eat the right foods and that their water stays pure. You will also have to change the water and clean the tank regularly.

You will need to scrape the tank glass when you clean

Taking your hobby further

Once you have learnt to keep cold-water fish, you may want to start to keep warm-water fish from all over the world. You can even create a natural habitat in a tank and fill it with the colourful fish from that wild habitat.

A community warm-water tank will contain fish from all over the world

People to help

The best fish-keeper always tries to find out more about his pets. You can ask your vet or an aquarist how to keep your fish healthy and happy.

You will sometimes need to visit your vet

Part of the family

Everyone will want to watch your fish swimming about in their tank and will be interested in what they do.

Beware!
You must ask an adult to help you with any of the electrical equipment.

Ask a grown-up
When you see this sign, you should ask an adult to help you.

Things to remember

When you keep fish, there are some important rules you must follow:

➤ Always switch off the electricity and unplug everything before working on your fish tank.

➤ Wash your hands after touching the tank water or anything inside the tank and feeding your fish.

➤ Don't tap the tank glass or annoy your fish.

➤ Follow instructions carefully when fitting electrical equipment.

What is a fish?

Fish belong to a very large group of animals called vertebrates, which means that they have a skull and an internal skeleton made of bone or gristle. Unlike most vertebrates, fish live in water. They are able to breath under water through gills, and move around using fins. Their skin is usually covered in scales to protect them. Fish are cold-blooded, which means that their bodies are the same temperature as the water around them.

Large eye sees all around

Soft, fleshy mouth

Hole for water to leave the gills

Caudal fin on end of tail

Jawless lamprey

Backbone made of gristle

Cartilaginous thornback ray

Kinds of fish

There are three main types of fish. One type, called jawless, have a fleshy sucker mouth instead of a jaw. Cartilaginous fish, like sharks and rays, have a rubbery skeleton made of gristle. Bony fish have a skeleton made of bone.

Skin contains hard scales

Strong mouth has a bony jaw

Bony tinfoil barb

Inside a fish

Some fish have skin that is almost transparent, so you can see inside them. Look at all the fine bones. The thick backbone runs along the middle of the body. You can also see the swim bladder. This sack, full of air, helps the fish to stay at different water depths.

Gills

Swim bladder

Backbone

Glass catfish

Stomach

Fin bones are called rays

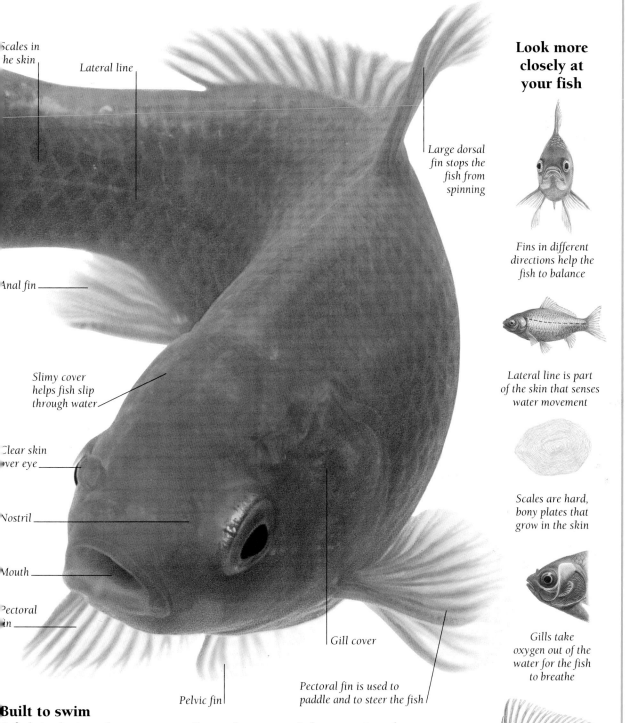

Scales in
the skin

Lateral line

Large dorsal
fin stops the
fish from
spinning

Anal fin

Slimy cover
helps fish slip
through water

Clear skin
over eye

Nostril

Mouth

Pectoral
fin

Pelvic fin

Gill cover

Pectoral fin is used to
paddle and to steer the fish

Look more closely at your fish

Fins in different
directions help the
fish to balance

Lateral line is part
of the skin that senses
water movement

Scales are hard,
bony plates that
grow in the skin

Gills take
oxygen out of the
water for the fish
to breathe

Delicate fins with
thin rays are used
for steering

Built to swim

A fish is designed to move easily under water. It has a pointed
head and a smooth, streamlined body. The goldfish swims
forwards by moving its body and big tail from side to side.
The fins are used for steering and help to keep the fish stable.

Life in the wild

Seas and oceans, rivers, lakes, streams and ponds are all types of water environment. Some have cold water, others have warm water. Some are fast-flowing, but others are still. All these kinds of water contain fish. The fish have developed the best ways of swimming, communicating, eating and hiding from their enemies in the water environment that they live in.

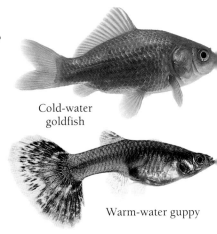

Cold-water goldfish

Warm-water guppy

Warm and cold water
Some fish, like goldfish, live in fresh, cold water. Others, like guppies, come from warm water. The temperature of a fish is the same as the water it lives in. Sudden cold or warmth may kill it.

Salmon

Marine and freshwater
Marine fish live in the salty waters of the sea. Most other fish live in freshwater ponds, inland rivers and lakes. A few fish, like the salmon, can survive in both salt and fresh water. When salmon want to breed, they leave the salty sea and swim up freshwater rivers.

Freshwater cobalt blue cichlid

Tail flicks from side to side

Caudal fin is still

Fin is held away from body to steady the fish

Body is straight when the fish is resting

Spot looks like the eye of a big fish to confuse an enemy

Twinspot wrasse digs into gravel

Surviving in different landscapes

Fish have learnt to hide from enemies between rocks and plants. Where there is sand, some fish dig a hole to hide in.

Pectoral fin is used to steer

Slimy skin coating protects the fish from infection

Showing feelings

Fish tell each other how they feel by changing their looks or smell, or acting in a special way. These two kissing gouramis look like friends. In fact, they are arguing.

Pelvic fin is not used in swimming

Dorsal fin helps to stop the fish twisting

Moving in water

Fish have a very muscular body and tail to push themselves through water. Like many other fish of the same shape, goldfish swim by curving their bodies and sweeping their tails powerfully from side to side.

Pointed head pushes through the water

Body curves from side to side when the fish is swimming

Stopping to sleep

Most fish rest by staying still for several hours. Some marine fish bury themselves in sand. Many cartilaginous fish never stop moving, even when they sleep.

Eye has no eyelid to close while resting

Fish lie together in a row

Clown loach

All shapes and colours

Over many millions of years, fish have adapted to life in the world's waters. They have developed special features to protect themselves from their enemies. Chinese people were the first to keep goldfish as pets. They bred the fish with strange features to create "fancy" goldfish. These fish are not as tough, or easy to look after, as the common goldfish.

Fish can dart away to avoid enemies

Cardinal tetras

Fish detects change in direction of group

Bullet-shaped for fast swimming

Long, thin fish with pointed heads swim swiftly and change direction easily. They often swim together in large numbers, or shoals. Their enemies are too confused by the shoal to attack one of them.

Amazing shape change

Fish that live alone are not protected by a shoal. When a porcupine fish is frightened, it puts up its prickles, and swells up by taking in water.

Upright spikes are sharp   Porcupine fish

Spines lie flat against body

Colour camouflage

Look for the fish in the picture. Some fish are the same colour and shape as their surroundings so that enemies can't see them.

Fins grasp the weed like little hands   Sargassum fish

Black and yellow signal danger in nature

Puffed-up fish looks like an underwater hedgehog

Mandarin fish

Yellow spots

Green dots break up fish outline

Blue stripes on fin

Bright orange lines dazzle as tail moves

The stubby fantail has two tail fins

The large fins of the veiltail make it a weak swimmer

Dazzling colours

In some waters, fish are brilliant colours. Orange, green and blue hide this fish in a coral reef. Spots and stripes break up a fish's outline to baffle its enemies.

Hatchet fish

Back is dull

Dark above, light below

Many fish have dark backs. From the sky, they blend into the water, so birds cannot spot them. But their undersides are silver. Seen by their enemies below, they look like the sky.

Underside is light and shiny

The moor is a black veiltail with very large eyes

Fish is brightly coloured in its natural home

Ram fish

Thickened scales on the pearscale have white centres

Changing colours

Well-camouflaged mudskipper

Lots of fish can disguise themselves by turning different colours. They become the colour that most closely matches their background.

Fish turns pale in light conditions

The celestial has been bred with upturned eyes so it can't see forwards

Walking fish

Using specially shaped fins as legs, some fish skip across mud. They have a water bubble on their gills for air. They breathe extra air through their mouth lining and skin.

A bubble-eye has water sacks under its eyes

15

Things you will need

Your fish will need a tank to live in. Buy stones and plants to put in the tank so that you can make your pets' underwater home interesting. You must also get some special things to keep the tank clean and the fish healthy. Ask a grown-up to help you choose the right kind of water filter and to wire all the electrical equipment. Get everything ready before you go to choose your fish.

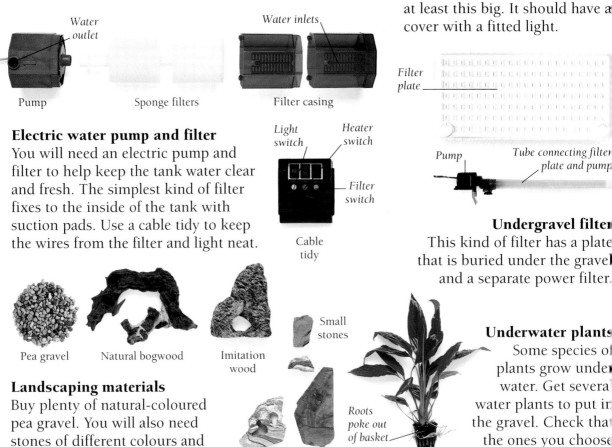

Width
30 cm
(12 in)

40 cm
(15 in)

← 60 cm (24 in) →

Large, glass tank
Look at the measurements in the picture. Your tank must be at least this big. It should have a cover with a fitted light.

Water outlet

Water inlets

Pump

Sponge filters

Filter casing

Electric water pump and filter
You will need an electric pump and filter to help keep the tank water clear and fresh. The simplest kind of filter fixes to the inside of the tank with suction pads. Use a cable tidy to keep the wires from the filter and light neat.

Light switch

Heater switch

Filter switch

Cable tidy

Filter plate

Pump

Tube connecting filter plate and pump

Undergravel filter
This kind of filter has a plate that is buried under the gravel and a separate power filter.

Pea gravel

Natural bogwood

Imitation wood

Small stones

Landscaping materials
Buy plenty of natural-coloured pea gravel. You will also need stones of different colours and sizes. Get interesting-shaped pieces of real or imitation wood.

Rock with holes

Large piece of slate

Roots poke out of basket

Broad-leaved plant

Underwater plants
Some species of plants grow under water. Get several water plants to put in the gravel. Check that the ones you choose are healthy and easy to look after (see p22)

Fish foods

Make sure that you buy some all-in-one, dried fish food, called "complete". This contains everything your pets will need to stay healthy. Fresh food, such as lettuce, and live food, can be fed as a treat.

Airtight tub of dried food

Complete dried fish flakes

Live water fleas

Scouring pad

Polishing pad

Magnetic glass scraper

Scrubbing brush

Sponge

Scissors

Bucket to hold cleaning water

Sieve

Small net

Large net

Water equipment

Tap water contains chemicals that will harm your pets. Buy a bucket and special liquids to prepare the water for your fish. Get a siphon to transfer water in and out of the tank. You will need a plate to pour water onto when you are filling the tank.

Filter starter

Measuring cup

Tap water conditioner

Small plate

Cleaning equipment

You will need special equipment to keep everything clean and tidy. Buy a sieve to wash gravel, a brush to scrub rocks, and a scraper and cloth to clean the tank glass. Get scissors to prune the plants, and fine nets to catch floating leaves.

Plunge-start siphon with gravel cleaner

Bucket to hold tank water

Water testing

Your fish are very sensitive to the temperature and freshness of the water they live in. You will need a water quality test kit and thermometers to keep a check on the water (see p30).

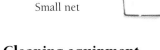

Water quality test kit

Tank thermometer

Bucket thermometer

Setting up your fish tank

Put your tank on a strong base in a sheltered position. Before you start to fill it, decide where you want all the stones and pieces of wood to go. A good design hides the filter and has space for the fish to swim freely. The things for the tank must be washed and the water specially prepared. Ask an adult to connect the electric cables.

Turn the wood to soak every part

1 Soak the bogwood. Th water will turn brown. Change the water every two days until it stays clea

2 Clean the tank and all the equipment. Wash sharp-edged slates in the bucket. Do not use any detergent. When everything is clean, rinse out the tank with fresh water.

3 Half-fill your sieve with gravel. Pour water into the sieve until it runs out clear. Wash enough gravel to fill your tank up to seven centimetres (three inches).

An apron will keep your clothes dry

Bucket to catch the dirty water

Shake the sieve so the water reaches every stone

Scrub the filter casing

Cleaned filter left to dry

Thermometer should be wiped with the cloth

Heavy stones must not be dropped

Use the bucket to wash things with jagged edges

4 Gently pour the clean gravel into the tank. Press the gravel so it slopes from the back o the front. Fish waste and dead plant eaves will then collect at the front.

Sieve to carry the gravel

Use your hand to shape the gravel

Fix the filter to a back corner

Black and

5 Attach the filter to the tank so the spout is level with the bottom of the band. When the tank is full, the spout will be at the water level.

Suction cups stick the filter to the glass

cm (3 in) of ravel at the back

5 cm (2 in) of gravel at the front

6 **Ask an adult to wire** the electric cables from he filter and the light nto the cable tidy. Plug he cable tidy into a wall socket, but do not turn it on yet.

Light cable

Cable tidy cable

Filter cable

Switch for light

Switch for pump

Where to site the tank

Place the tank on a sturdy cabinet that doesn't shake

Keep the tank away from bright sunshine

Do not put the tank near a radiator

Make sure the tank is out of draughts

Keep the tank out of reach of cats and other pets

Continued on next page

7 **Put the slates** in front of the filter, then position the other stones. Push them well into the gravel so they can't fall over. Make sure you leave your fish a lot of space to swim in. Create some hiding places for them.

Tall slates hide the filter

Place the stone firmly in the gravel

Scoop a small hole for the stone

Wooden arch for your fish to swim through

Hold the slate steady with one hand

Tree-shaped piece of wood for fish to swim around

Water flows along tube

Plunge the pump vigorously in the bucket of conditioned water to start the siphon

8 **Position the pieces of wood** to finish decorating the tank. Make sure each piece is pushed deep into the gravel, so it cannot float to the surface of the water.

Water in the bucket must be higher than water in the tank

Rubber cup sticks thermometer to glass

9 **Fix the thermometer** to the front of the tank, where you can read it easily. Press the rubber suction cup firmly up against the glass to hold the thermometer in place.

Upturned bucket makes a good stand

    Continued from page 19

10 **Prepare the tap water** to fill your tank. You must add conditioner to every bucketful. Read the bottle label to find out how much conditioner to use.

Use the cup to measure out the right amount of conditioner

11 **Fill one third** of your fish tank with the conditioned water. Put the pump-end of the siphon into the bucket of water and hold the other end over the plate in the tank. Plunge the pump-end up and down until the water flows.

Bottle of conditioner

Bucket contains fresh tap water

Use the tube to stir in the conditioner

Plate spreads water so gravel is not disturbed

Decorative background
You can draw a vivid underwater scene to stick to the back of your tank.

Use waterproof pens in case your picture is splashed

Adding the plants

You can now put your plants in the tank and fill it to the top. The plants will help to keep your fish healthy by making oxygen for them to breathe and by feeding on the fish waste. Your fish will also like to shelter among the leaves. Don't worry if they nibble them – plants are good food.

Plants for a cold-water tank
Use these pictures to help you choose the types and numbers of plants to buy for your tank.

Tiny curly leaves on long stem

Cut plant stem will grow roots when planted

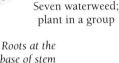

Seven waterweed; plant in a group

Roots at the base of stem

Seven water star plants

Twisting stem with small leaves

One Ludwigia natans plant

Long, thin leaves look like reeds

Ten straight eel grass; plant in a clump

Roots are in a basket

Healthy leaf is bright green

One peace lily in a basket

Leaf is red underneath

Six cardinal flower plants; put in two groups

Handle the roots carefully

1 **Wash the plants gently** to remove any dirt or small animals such as snails. If the roots are very long, trim them with a pair of scissors to about two centimetres (one inch) long. Keep the washed plants in water until you are ready to put them in the tank. This will stop them wilting.

Dirty plants ready for washing

Clean plants soak in water on a tray

2 **Before you start to plant**, plan where to put the plants. Group them into clumps, choosing taller ones for the back of the tank. Dig small holes in the gravel to put the roots in. Push the gravel back around the roots.

Put short plants at the front of the tank

3 **Fill the tank up** to the top with conditioned water (see p21) when you have finished planting.

Fill with water up to the black band

4 👥**Ask a grown-up to help** you work out how much filter starter to add to the tank. This special liquid helps the filter to start working properly.

Use two fingers to make a deep hole in the gravel

Aim the jet onto the glass so the gravel isn't disturbed

5 👥**Now you can put on** the lid and turn on the pump and light. Remember you must have dry hands before you touch any of the switches. Leave the pump running all the time. Turn the light on every morning and off every evening.

Plants look bright under light

Groups of plants look best

Stems are held upright by water

Tall plants help to hide the filter

Choosing your fish

You can keep up to five small goldfish or six community cold-water fish in the tank shown on page 16. If you have a larger tank, ask an aquarist to help you work out how many fish you can keep. Get one or two fish every two weeks. This gives the bacteria that destroy the harmful wastes time to grow in your tank.

Young fish is still small

Old fish is very large

Oversized
In a large tank, fish will grow very big. Don't buy fish that are longer than seven centimetres (three inches) for your tank.

Where to get your fish
✦ A friend may have fish
✦ A fish-keeper's club
✦ An aquarist's shop
✦ An animal shelter

Partial water change removes nitrates

Fish produces ammonia waste

Nitrates collect in tank water

Bacteria turns ammonia into nitrites, then nitrates

The nitrogen cycle
Useful bacteria grow in a filter and in gravel. They convert harmful waste produced by fish into salts, called nitrites and nitrates. Regular changes of some of the tank water will remove any wastes and salts.

Choosing goldfish
You can keep as many as five goldfish in your tank.

Common goldfish

Shubunkin

Calico fantail

Comet

Sarasa comet

Hardy first fish
Get a common goldfish and a comet when your filter has been running for two days.

Two weeks later
After two weeks, add a shubunkin and a sarasa comet.

Least hardy last
Wait two weeks before adding a calico fantail. This fish is most sensitive to new water.

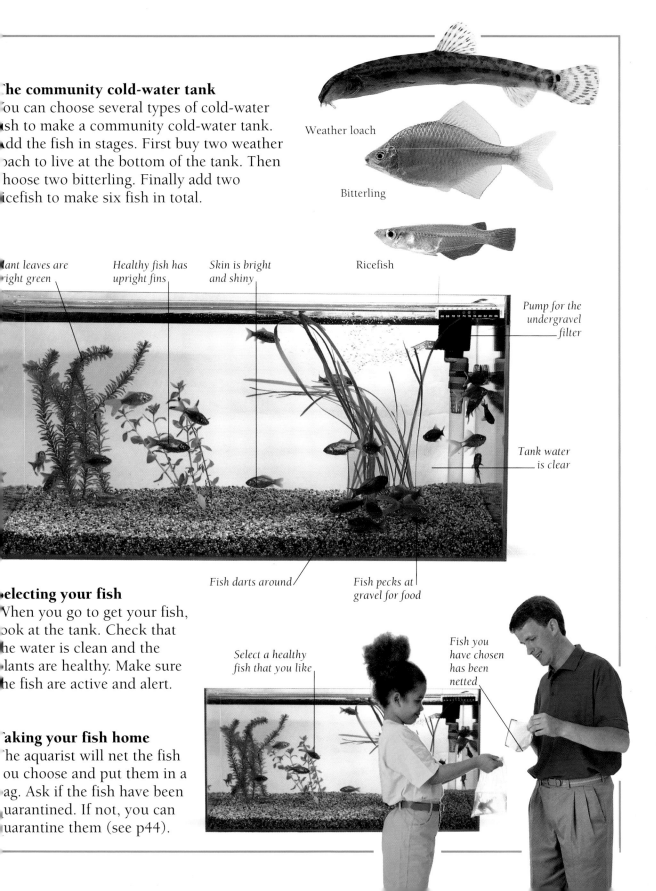

The community cold-water tank

You can choose several types of cold-water fish to make a community cold-water tank. Add the fish in stages. First buy two weather loach to live at the bottom of the tank. Then choose two bitterling. Finally add two ricefish to make six fish in total.

Weather loach

Bitterling

Ricefish

Plant leaves are bright green

Healthy fish has upright fins

Skin is bright and shiny

Pump for the undergravel filter

Tank water is clear

Fish darts around

Fish pecks at gravel for food

Selecting your fish

When you go to get your fish, look at the tank. Check that the water is clean and the plants are healthy. Make sure the fish are active and alert.

Taking your fish home

The aquarist will net the fish you choose and put them in a bag. Ask if the fish have been quarantined. If not, you can quarantine them (see p44).

Select a healthy fish that you like

Fish you have chosen has been netted

Welcome home

The water in the bag that you bring your new fish home in is a different temperature and quality to the water in your tank. If you put your fish straight into their tank they will become ill. Follow these steps to make sure that your fish adjust to their new home. Remember that you will need to wait at least two weeks before you add any more fish.

Lift the li with both hand

1 Before lifting off the lid, turn off the filter and light and unplug the cable tidy.

The bag is still sealed

Carefully place the bag of fish in your tank

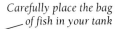

2 Float the bag of fish in your tank. Leave it for at least twenty minutes so that the temperature of the water in the bag reaches the same temperature as the water in your tank.

Hold your thermometer in the middle of the bag

3 Check **the temperature** of the bag water after opening the bag and rolling down the sides. Read the temperature shown on your tank thermometer. Only go onto the next step when both thermometers read the same.

4 Scoop some water from the tank into a jug and pour it gently into the open bag of fish. Wait about five minutes and then add some more. By slowly mixing water from the tank into the bag your fish will adjust to their new water.

Pour the water slowly so that the fish aren't disturbed

Try not to let any dirty bag water spill into the tank

Fine mesh net will not damage the fish's scales or fins

Released fish explores new surroundings

Fish swims under wood bridge

Filter is now switched back on

5 Put your small net into the bag. As soon as a fish swims into the net, lift it out and put it straight into the tank. Gently tilt the net so the fish can swim out on its own.

6 Put the lid back on the tank and switch on the filter. Leave the light off until the next day so that the fish can get some rest.

✦ **Adding more fish**
After releasing your new fish into your tank, you must wait at least two weeks for the tank to settle, or mature, before adding any more fish. Check that the fish you want to add to your tank have already been quarantined (see p44).

Feeding your fish

Your fish nibble the tank plants and the algae that grow on the inside of the tank. But they need other food to keep them healthy. You should buy complete flake food that is specially made for fish to give to them most days. Do not give too much food because any uneaten food will rot and make the tank water poisonous. You can buy special food tablets to put in your fish tank when you go on holiday (see p45).

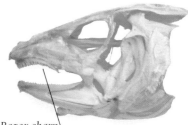

Razor-sharp teeth grip prey   Atlantic cod skul

Feeding in the wild
Most fish eat both plants and other animals. Some fish, like Atlantic cod, eat mainly meat. They have sharp teeth for biting and grinding.

Mid-feeding forceps fish

Upturned mouth for snapping floating insects

Surface-feeding archer fish

Long, thin mouth for pinching food out of rock crevices

Feeding from top to bottom
Some fish, like goldfish, live in all depths of water. Their mouths face forward so they can feed anywhere. Other fish live at one water depth. They have developed special mouths to feed at these levels.

Down-turned mouth vacuums along the floor

Bottom-feeding catfish

Sensitive barbels feel for food

The staple diet

Give your fish a specially prepared all-in-one flake food that contains all the goodness they need.

Feed only a small pinch of flakes

Complete fish flakes

When to feed

Feed your fish every morning and evening. To make sure your fish are not overfed, don't feed them for one day every fortnight.

Sprinkle the flakes over the water surface

Flakes float on the surface, then sink

Ricefish feeds at the surface

Bitterling is a mid-feeder

Weather loach feeds on the bottom

Label shows how much to feed

Floating sticks

Food tablets

Freeze-dried tubifex worms

Frozen bloodworms

An interesting treat

Once a week, instead of flakes, feed floating sticks or press one tablet onto the side of the tank.

Blanched lettuce leaf

Fresh lettuce leaf

Live food

Buy frozen, freeze-dried or fresh live food to feed to your fish once a week instead of flakes.

Fresh green food

👭If your fish eat the plants, give them a lettuce leaf dipped in hot water. Do not leave the leaf in the tank for more than 12 hours.

Goldfish nibble at the water's surface looking for flakes

Watching eating habits

Your fish should start to eat as soon as you feed them. Goldfish quickly learn to come to the surface when you lift the lid of the tank. Never overfeed your fish, although it is fun watching them gobble up food and dart about looking for more.

Caring for your tank

You must look after your tank to keep the fish and plants healthy. Turn on the light every morning; remember to switch it off before you go to bed. Twice a day, feed your fish (see p29) and check the water temperature. When you first get your tank, do a nitrite test every day.

Reading should stay the same

Upright fin shows fish is well

Eye sparkles

Plant leaves look healthy

Water is clear

Shiny, smooth gold scales

Fish darts around quickly

Checking the temperature
Read the water temperature on the thermometer and write it down twice a day. If the temperature often changes check the tank is not in a draught or near a heater.

Everyday attention
Check the tank every morning. Make sure the filter is working, the water is clean, and the fish look shiny and are swimming about.

Add drops of test liquid to sample of tank water

Colour on card shows nitrite level

Sample water colours

Testing for nitrites
⇧⇧Ammonia in fish waste is converted into nitrites that build up in new tank water. Large amounts of nitrites will harm your fish. Use a special kit to test for nitrites. Carefully read the instructions. Test every day for two weeks after you set up the tank.

Reading the test
The test water will colour. Compare the colour with the test card to see if the water is safe. Do a partial water change if it is unsafe (see p32).

Cleaning the tank

Your fish and plants will become ill in a dirty tank. Use the siphon to vacuum the gravel and remove dirty water. Clean the glass with the scraper. Save old water to wash the filter in. Refill the tank with conditioned water.

Gently wipe the condensation tray

Grime stops light reaching the plants

When to do a water change

➡ Every two weeks.

➡ When the nitrite level in the water is too high.

➡ Whenever the tank water looks cloudy.

1 **Clean the plastic condensation tray.** Switch off the light and filter and unplug the cable tidy. Lift off the lid. Wipe the dirt off the condensation tray with a damp sponge.

Dirty water runs down siphon tube

Bucket must be lower than tank so water can flow

Gravel is washed as water flows up siphon

2 **Start a partial water change** by taking out one tenth of the tank water. Move your siphon around the gravel at the front of the tank, where the fish waste collects.

Cut the plants when the fish are far away

3 **Prune any plants** that are too tall. Cut them back with your scissors. Snip off any brown, dying leaves. Replace any unhealthy-looking plants.

Continued on next page

The handle and the scraper have magnets so they move together

4 **Scrape the green slime**, called algae, off the front and sides of the inside of the glass with the scraper. If you let the algae grow, you will not be able to see your fish. Leave the algae on the glass at the back of your tank. It is a healthy food.

5 **Pull off the filter casing** after taking the filter out of the tank. Remove the dirty filter sponges. Wash the filter casing thoroughly.

Carefully take off the casing

Remember to wash each part

6 **Rinse out the filter sponges** in the water that you have saved. By doing this, you will not kill the bacteria that live in the sponges, which help to clean the water.

Squeeze the sponge gently to wash out the dirt

Move the siphon all around the tank

Bucket filled with the old tank water

7 **Siphon out** another five centimetres (two inches) of water from the tank. This sucks up the mess made when you pruned the plants and scraped off the algae.

8 Prepare tap water to refill your tank by conditioning it (see p21). Stir in the conditioner using the end of your siphon.

Read the thermometer carefully

Conditioner

9 Measure the temperature of the conditioned water. When the tank thermometer and the bucket thermometer read the same, you can add the new water to your tank.

10 Either use the jug or the siphon to refill the tank to the top. Dry your hands before putting on the lid and switching the filter and light back on.

Pour water over a plate so it doesn't disturb the fish

✦ Moving your tank
Never try to move a full tank or it will break. Empty all the water out of your tank before lifting it. Your fish can stay in some of the old water in a bucket.

Your pet care check list
Use this list to keep a record of all the jobs you need to do.

Copy this chart. Tick the jobs off when you have finished them.

Every day:
Count your fish

Watch to see if your fish are active

Check the filter is working

Read the water temperature

Turn lights on in the morning and off in the evening

Feed your fish

Do a nitrite test on a new tank

◆

Every two weeks:
Do a nitrite test on a mature tank

Partially change the tank water

Clean the gravel

Wipe the lid

Prune the plants

Scrape off the algae

Wash the filter

◆

Every year:
Re-arrange the tank

Ask an adult to help you check the tank electrics

The outdoor fish

A pond is a natural home for tough cold-water fish like the common goldfish. If you have a garden, you may have enough space to make your own pond. Goldfish can grow very big in a pond, so it must be at least three metres (four yards) long. Buy a large, deep pond liner that has a shallow shelf to put plants on. You can ask at your vet centre for more information about building and looking after a pond.

Tall thin reeds

Variegated sweet flag

Big, flat leaves provide shade for fish

Water lily

Hardy common goldfish

Water milfoil

Water is 60 cm (2 ft) deep at this end

Pond weed

Fish looks for a place to rest between plant pots

Gravel contains useful bacteria

Layer of sand protects the pond liner

Sharp stone is buried by sand

Flowering rush

Marsh marigold

Tough polythene pond liner

Pond life

Buy plants that grow in or around water to put in the pond. Put some of them around the edge and stand some on the pond floor. Get six hardy common goldfish to put in the pond. You will need to change some of the water once a year.

Large pond net

Flake food   Floating sticks

Water conditioner   Algae controller

Extra equipment

Get a large net to catch your goldfish and to scoop any leaves off the water surface. You will have to buy special chemicals to keep the pond water healthy and food for the fish and plants.

Setting up a warm-water tank

Fish that live in warm water in the wild can be kept as pets. When you have learnt how to look after cold-water fish, you may want to set up a warm-water or tropical tank. Use the same equipment, and follow the same steps as you did for a cold-water tank. You will also need a tank heater and tropical plants and fish food.

Heating the tank
Buy a heater that is the right size for your tank. Get one with a thermostat that switches the heater off when the water is the right temperature.

Tropical fish food

Buy a complete flake food specially made for tropical fish. Feed a pinch every morning and evening (see p29).

Treat foods
Give your tropical fish a treat food instead of flake food once a week. Some treat foods can help keep your fish brightly coloured. Bottom-feeding fish enjoy tablets that sink.

Flakes   Tablets

Granules   Flakes

Plant food
A liquid plant food gives your plants the goodness they need to grow. Follow the instructions carefully.

Getting the plants
Buy the types and numbers of warm-water plants that are shown in the picture. Make sure all of the plants you choose are healthy.

pH test
Tropical fish live in acid, alkaline and neutral water. Get a pH test kit to find out if the water in your tank is acid, alkaline or neutral.

Sample cup

Indicator

One broad-leaf Amazon sword   Eight dwarf Hygrophila

Five twisted eel grass   Six dwarf Cryptocoryne   Four water wisteria

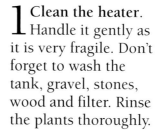
Wipe the glass carefully

1 **Clean the heater.** Handle it gently as it is very fragile. Don't forget to wash the tank, gravel, stones, wood and filter. Rinse the plants thoroughly.

2 👥 **Ask an adult** to help you attach the heater to the tank and wire it into the cable tidy. Set the thermostat to 24° C (77° F). Do not switch the heater on until the tank is full of water.

Plant the stems in a group

Fix the heater at the height shown in the instructions

Washed gravel slopes from back to front

3 **Add the plants** after you have put in gravel, stones and wood. It is easiest to plant them when your tank is one third full of conditioned water.

4 **Read the thermometer** when the tank is full and the heater and filter are switched on. The temperature should slowly go up, then stay at 24°C (77°F).

Small sample of water scooped out of the tank

5 👥 **To do a pH test**, take some water out of the tank in the sample cup. Follow the test instructions carefully. You will need to add drops of the indicator to the water in the cup.

6 **The water will change colour**. To find out the pH, compare the water colour to the colours on the test card. Write down the result for your aquarist.

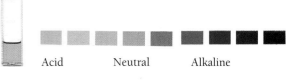

Acid   Neutral   Alkaline

A community warm-water tank

It is easiest to start to keep tropical fish in a community warm-water tank. The fish for this tank come from neutral waters all over the world. They can be kept together happily as they live at different water depths. Follow the steps on page 26 when you put new fish in the tank. Make sure the temperature of the water in the bag and the tank are the same before releasing a fish.

The first fortnight
Put the first fish in the tank after it has been set up for two days. For two weeks, do regular partial water changes to remove nitrites and check the water is still neutral.

Sunset platy nibbles at the water's surface

Heater is hidden by tall, twisting reeds

Sunset platy

Bronze corydorus

Male rosy barb

Female guppy

Male guppy has beautiful brightly coloured tail

Female rosy barb

Male guppy

Bottom-feeding bronze corydorus looks for food in gravel

Adding fish to the tank
First get a male and female South American sunset platy. After two weeks add a pair of Indian rosy barbs.

The next stage
The third group of fish to put in are four South American bronze corydorus or catfish. Two weeks later, add a male and female guppy.

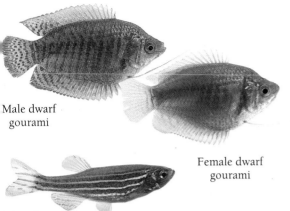

Male dwarf
gourami

Female dwarf
gourami

Zebra danio

The final fish

Wait another two weeks before buying one
male and one female Indian dwarf gourami.
The last fish that you should add to the tank
are four Indian zebra danios.

The finished tank

Your completed warm-water tank is home for
16 tropical fish. You will soon learn which fish
live at each depth. Watch the tank at night,
and you will see the shy catfish become active.

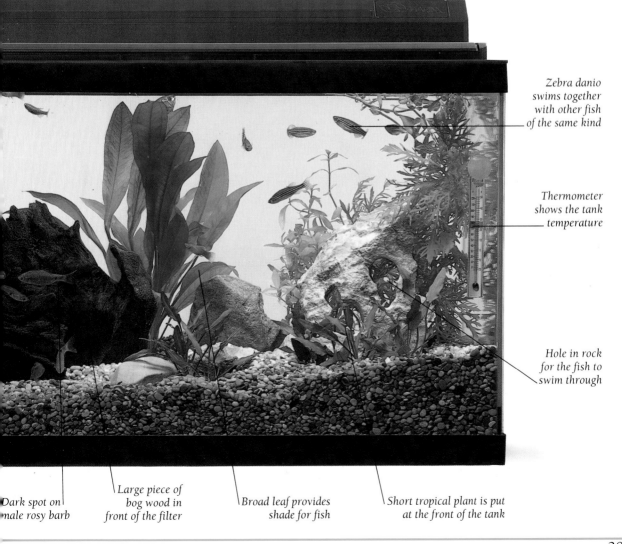

*Zebra danio
swims together
with other fish
of the same kind*

*Thermometer
shows the tank
temperature*

*Hole in rock
for the fish to
swim through*

*Dark spot on
male rosy barb*

*Large piece of
bog wood in
front of the filter*

*Broad leaf provides
shade for fish*

*Short tropical plant is put
at the front of the tank*

Theme tanks

When you become an experienced fish-keeper you can set up a theme tank with alkaline or acid water. This is a home for fish that come from one habitat, like a rocky lake in East Africa, or an Amazon rainforest stream. Landscape your tank to look like a small part of that wild place.

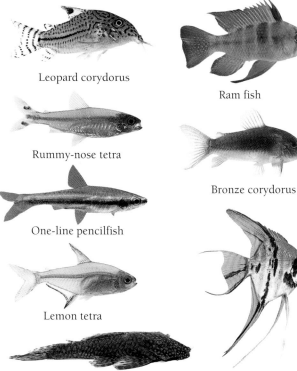

Leopard corydorus

Ram fish

Rummy-nose tetra

Bronze corydorus

One-line pencilfish

Lemon tetra

Bristle-nosed catfish

Angelfish

Fish for an Amazon tank

Get four of each type of fish shown in the pictures. Some of these fish live at each depth of the tank. In the wild, they live in the acid streams that flow through the rainforest into the Amazon river.

Lush jungle grows above
Amazon stream

Amazon rainforest tank

Your Amazon tank must be at least 100 cm (36 in) long. Set it up in the same way as the warm-water tank. Ask your aquarist how to make the tank water slightly acid. Use bogwood to make the tank look like an Amazon stream.

*Bright stripes
on ram fish*

*Leopard corydorus
has black spots*

*Fin on the angelfish
is pointed*

*Bristle-nosed catfish
swims along the bottom*

Large, flat rock is carefully positioned

Female kennyi cichlid has orange stripes

Female zebra cichlid is blotchy

Cave formed from rocks

Deep layer of coral sand

East African rocky lake tank

This theme tank should be at least 130 cm (48 in) long. Landscape the tank with coral sand and rocky caves where fish can hide. You don't need any plants. You will need to make the water very slightly alkaline.

The shores of Lake Malawi

Fish for an East African tank

The pictures show you the kinds of fish you will need for this tank. Get a pair of each type. Lake Malawi fish are very brightly coloured. They live in small rocky areas in slightly alkaline waters near the lake shore. In the pictures, males are always shown in front of the females.

Johanni cichlid

Red-topped zebra

Cobalt blue cichlid

Livingstone's cichlid

Blue zebra danio

Kennyi cichlid

Orange blotch zebra cichlid

Ornatus cichlid

41

The growing fish

Baby fish are called fry. Some fish have live fry that can swim. Other fish produce eggs that hatch in water. Most pet fish are not able to rear fry in a tank unless you give them special conditions to live in. You must think very carefully before you decide to try to breed fish. If you are successful, you will need to find good homes for a large number of new fish.

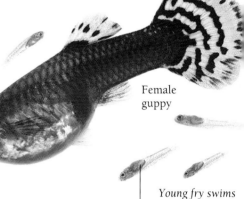

Female guppy

Young fry swims alongside its mother

Live-bearing fish
A mother live-bearing fish has eggs which hatch inside her. You can sometimes see the eye-spots of young fry. When the fry are born, they swim with their mother.

Protective bubble nest
Before mating, some fish blow bubbles at the water surface. When the female produces eggs, the male collects them in his mouth and spits them into the bubbles. He will guard the eggs

Bubble protects eggs

Male fish keeps watch over the nest

Siamese fighting fish

Fry is still safe in its mother's mouth

Mouthbrooding cichlid

Fry must now look after themselves

Mouthbrooding fish
Some fish from the cichlid family carry the eggs of their young in their mouths. Even after they have hatched, the fry may go back into their mother's mouth for safety.

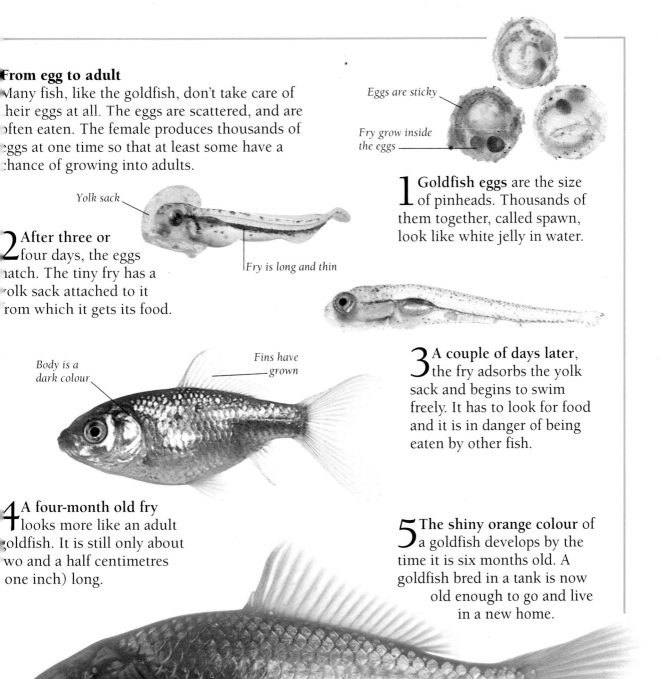

From egg to adult

Many fish, like the goldfish, don't take care of their eggs at all. The eggs are scattered, and are often eaten. The female produces thousands of eggs at one time so that at least some have a chance of growing into adults.

Eggs are sticky

Fry grow inside the eggs

1 **Goldfish eggs** are the size of pinheads. Thousands of them together, called spawn, look like white jelly in water.

Yolk sack

2 **After three or** four days, the eggs hatch. The tiny fry has a yolk sack attached to it from which it gets its food.

Fry is long and thin

Body is a dark colour

Fins have grown

3 **A couple of days later**, the fry adsorbs the yolk sack and begins to swim freely. It has to look for food and it is in danger of being eaten by other fish.

4 **A four-month old fry** looks more like an adult goldfish. It is still only about two and a half centimetres (one inch) long.

5 **The shiny orange colour** of a goldfish develops by the time it is six months old. A goldfish bred in a tank is now old enough to go and live in a new home.

Scales in bright orange skin

The healthy fish

You need to look after your fish properly to make sure they stay healthy. You must give them the right food (see p29), change the water regularly and keep the tank clean (p31). If a fish looks different or is acting strangely, separate it from the other fish in a quarantine tank.

Pea gravel

Plastic tank

Plastic plant

Imitation wood

➤ People who can help
The vets and nurses at your local vet centre will give you advice about how to look after your pets. An aquarist may also be able to help you with any questions about your fish.

Quarantine equipment
Quarantine a fish in a small tank. Put in pea gravel, plastic plants and imitation wood to make your fish feel at home.

Use the tank to take fish to your vet centre

Catching the fish
Move the large net around the tank until the fish swims close to it. Move the small net behind the fish to encourage it into the large net.

Isolated fish
Keep the fish you think is unwell in the tank until it looks better. You can use this tank to quarantine new fish that weren't quarantined by the breeder. Keep new fish in quarantine for two weeks.

Move the net gently

Fish swims into the large net

My pet's fact book

Try making a fact book about your tank with a page about each of your fish. Copy the headings on this page, or you can make up your own. Then write in the correct information about each fish.

Shubunkin

Calico fantail

Sarasa comet

Common goldfish

Comet

Leave a space at the beginning of the book to stick in a photograph or draw a picture of your tank. Then label all of your pet's special features.

Type of fish: **Common goldfish**

Date bought: **10th October**

Favourite food: **Floating sticks**

Best hiding place: **Wooden arch**

Vet's name: **Mark Evans**

Nurse's name: **Sarah Ponder**

Aquarist's name: **David Pool**

Going on holiday

You can buy holiday tablets to feed your fish if you are going away for more than a few days. Buy a time clock to switch the light on and off. It is a good idea to find someone to check your tank while you are away. If you are only away for a few days, your fish do not need feeding.

Index